WHAT IS LEGACY BOOK?

Legacy book is a simple do-it-yourself book designed for families to pass down for generations. Simply answer questions for each of the 9 chapters about YOUR life. Upon completion of the book, it can be gifted or given to family members to cherish and continue to pass down the family tree. Our mission through these books is to preserve and organize some of your memories, life lessons, interests, and life events. Keep in mind this book is not just a reflection of your life, but a tool to look forward for what's to come.

Think about it, what do you know about your great-great grandparents? Just as anyone else, you would probably love to know more about them. Please give your family the gift of LEGACY. Your children, grandchildren and so on will be very grateful you did.

DEDICATED TO

_____

TABLE OF CONTENTS

THE BASICS

CHAPTER 1

INSERT PICTURE

DATE: ___ / ___ / ___

WHAT IS YOUR NAME?

> ▶ When and where were you born?

....

....

....

....

▶ How would you describe yourself?

....

....

....

....

....

....

....

....

FAMILY ROOTS

CHAPTER 2

INSERT PICTURE

▶ Which countries are your ancestors from?

....

....

....

....

....

....

▶ What physical characteristics run in your family?

....

....

....

....

....

....

....

WHAT IS YOUR MOTHER'S NAME?

▶ Where is she from?

....

....

....

....

....

▶ Describe her

....

....

....

....

....

....

WHAT IS YOUR FATHER'S NAME?

▶ Where is he from?

....

....

....

....

....

▶ Describe him

....

....

....

....

....

....

▶ Do you have any siblings?

....

....

....

....

....

....

▶ What are their names and how much older/younger are they?

....

....

....

....

....

....

▶ What is the best memory you have with your siblings?

WHAT ARE YOUR MATERNAL GRANDPARENT'S NAMES?

▶ Where did they live?

....

....

....

....

....

▶ What was their role in your life?

....

....

....

....

....

....

....

WHAT ARE YOUR PATERNAL GRANDPARENT'S NAMES?

▶ Where did they live?

....

....

....

....

▶ What was their role in your life?

....

....

....

....

....

....

▶ Who were some of your closest outside relatives?

....

....

....

▶ What was your relationship with them like?

....

....

....

▶ What was dinner table conversation like growing up?

....

....

....

▶ What are some family traditions that you grew up with?

....

....

....

....

CHILDHOOD

CHAPTER 3

INSERT PICTURE

▶ Where did you attend elementary school?

....

....

▶ Where did you attend high school?

....

....

▶ What are some of your favorite school memories?

....

....

....

....

....

....

....

....

....

▶ What were you taught then that isn't taught now?

....

....

....

....

▶ What subjects did you like/dislike the most in school?

....

....

....

▶ Who were some of your favorite teachers and why?

....

....

....

....

....

....

▶ Who were some of your best friends growing up?

....

....

▶ What did you do for fun with your friends?

....

....

....

....

....

▶ Did you get into any trouble as a kid?

....

....

....

....

....

....

▶ Which childhood friendships continued into adulthood, if any?

....

....

....

....

....

....

▶ What were some notable major news events that occurred/affected you while growing up?

....

....

....

....

....

....

▶ How is the world different now?

....

....

....

....

▶ What were some of your favorite books growing up?

....

....

....

▶ What were some of your favorite TV shows and/or movies?

....

....

....

....

....

....

▶ What was your favorite music growing up?

....

....

....

....

▶ Did you have a job during your school years? If so, where at?

....

....

....

▶ Which extracurricular activities did you enjoy most growing up? (Ex. sports, band etc.)

....

....

....

....

....

....

▶ What were some of your hobbies growing up?

....

....

....

....

....

....

▶ Who did you look up to most as a kid? Why?

....

....

....

....

....

....

....

LOVE & MARRIAGE

CHAPTER 4

INSERT PICTURE

▶ Where did you first live as an adult?

....

....

....

▶ What did you do for fun as an adult?

....

....

....

....

▶ Where have you traveled?

....

....

....

....

....

▶ Who was your first love or significant other?

....

....

....

....

....

....

▶ What was the dating scene like at the time?

....

....

....

....

....

....

....

....

WHAT IS YOUR SPOUSE'S NAME?

▶ When and where was he/she born?

....

....

▶ Where did he/she grow up?

....

....

▶ When and how did you two first meet?

....

....

....

....

▶ What was your first date with him/her?

....

....

....

▶ When and where did you get married?

....

....

▶ Where did you first live with your significant other?

....

....

▶ What is a good memory from early marriage?

....

....

....

....

▶ Do you have any dating or love advice?

....

....

....

....

....

STARTING A FAMILY

CHAPTER 5

INSERT PICTURE

▶ What are the names of your kids (in order), and when and where were they born?

....

....

....

....

....

....

▶ How did life change when you became a parent?

....

....

....

....

....

....

....

▶ Did anyone unrelated become a part of your family?

....

....

....

▶ What is a favorite holiday memory?

....

....

....

....

▶ What are some fun things you love or loved to do with your family?

....

....

....

....

....

....

▶ What are some things that you're proud of your children for?

....

....

....

....

....

....

▶ What are the names of your grandkids (in order), and when were they born?

....

....

....

....

....

....

....

....

▶ How has life changed since becoming a grandparent?

....

....

....

....

....

....

▶ What is the best thing about having grandkids?

....

....

....

....

....

....

....

....

WORK AND CAREER

CHAPTER 6

INSERT PICTURE

► Were you ever in the military? If so, how was your experience?

....

....

....

....

....

► Can you name everywhere you worked?

....

....

....

....

....

....

....

....

▶ Which was your longest lasting job/career?

....

....

▶ As a kid, what did you want to be when you grew up?

....

....

▶ Did you ever start a business? If so, describe it.

....

....

....

▶ What were some major decisions or turning points in your career?

....

....

....

....

....

PASSIONS & PASSTIMES

CHAPTER 7

INSERT PICTURE

FAVORITES

TV Show

Movie

Food

Drink

Holiday

Sport

Book

▶ What are some of your favorite hobbies?

....

....

....

....

....

....

▶ What are some of your greatest talents?

....

....

....

....

....

....

....

FUTURE PLANS

C H A P T E R   8

INSERT PICTURE

▶ What are your goals for the future?

....

....

....

....

....

....

....

....

....

....

....

....

....

....

....

WORDS OF WISDOM ▬▬▬▬

CHAPTER 9

INSERT PICTURE

▶ What is the best advice you've ever taken?

....

....

....

....

....

....

▶ What is the best advice or life experienced lesson you could give someone?

....

....

....

....

....

....